Self-Discipline

The Ultimate Guide to Gain Self Confidence, Motivation, and Willpower You Need to Make Things Happen!

By

Jacob Wilson

© 2016

Table of Contents

Introduction 3

Step 1: Developing a Deep Sense of Self Awareness for Self-discipline 8

Step 2: Being Your True Self 11

Step 3: Setting Goals to Maximize Your Ability 14

Step 4: Being Honest with Yourself 20

Step 5: Find Your Motivation 25

Step 6: Develop Your Will Power 30

    1) Don't overwork your willpower. 31

    Many people use weight lifting to build their muscle, but they make sure they do not overwork them. You must do the same for your will power. Exercise your self-control and will power regularly. This strengthens it and, in turn, strengthens your self-discipline. However, make sure that you do not constantly deprive yourself or hurt your own willpower. This will just make things worse. Do not burn yourself out. If you burn yourself out, you will only make your self-confidence completely dwindle. 31

    2) Use your imagination. 32

    3) Build good habits for yourself. 32

    5) Stay away from temptations 33

Step 7: Break Old Habits 33

Step 8: Cultivate New Habits 36

Step 9: Track Your Progress..40
10 Day Challenge 44
Rewards for Being Self-Disciplined..................................44
Ten Day Start Plan for Self-Discipline.............................49
Conclusion: Enjoy Your New Self-discipline 53

Introduction

We all have dreams. But in order to make dreams come into reality, it takes an awful lot of determination, dedication, self-discipline, and effort.

-Jesse Owens

What is Self-discipline?

Self-discipline is what it takes to accomplish your dreams. Self-Discipline is vital to living a successful life. Self-discipline is the art of pushing yourself to go above and beyond without fear or laziness. Self-discipline is what it takes to get out of bed in the morning. Good self-discipline is what it takes to accomplish your small goals, like finishing an assignment or work project. Great self-discipline is what it takes to accomplish your dreams and your big goals like becoming the next American Ninja

Warrior or running a marathon. Self-discipline is vital, can honing this skill can improve your life beyond belief.

Self-discipline is Important and Beneficial

You need self-discipline even for the little things in life. Self-discipline is one of the most important and useful skills that you will find that you need in life; in fact, you will find, after reading this book that self-discipline is an important skill for everyone to possess. Those people who have the best self-discipline are those who are the most successful. This skill is essential and important in every part of life. Many people find self-discipline to be important, but not very many people take strides to strengthen it.

Although many people think of self-discipline as being harsh and strict with yourself, that is not really what it is. Self-discipline is not just about living a limited and restricted life. Self-discipline does not mean that you consistently deny yourself and make yourself happy. Instead, self-discipline means self-control, this is a sign of inner strength and a sign of the ability to control yourself, your actions, and your reactions. Self-discipline is important is reaching your goals and being the best you that you can possibly be. Having self-discipline gives you the ability to persevere with decisions and plans until you accomplish them. If you work hard enough, self-discipline will manifest itself as inner strength, this lets you overcome addictions, laziness, and procrastination. Self-discipline equals follow through.

Self-discipline helps you:

- Avoid acting rashly.
- Avoid Impulses.

- Keep promises that you make to yourself and others.
- Beat procrastination and laziness.
- Keep working even when motivation and enthusiasm has faded away.
- Do those things like exercise and wake up early that you know is good for you?
- Overcome bad habits.
- Keep calm, relaxed, and happy.

You can always start by doing a few things to help strengthen your resolve and self-discipline:

- Focus on understanding how important self-discipline is in your life.

- Be aware of your behavior and actions. Be aware of what you do when these behaviors and actions go undisciplined.
- Make a concerted effort to behave according to the decisions that you make and goals you set.

Step 1: Developing a Deep Sense of Self Awareness for Self-discipline

Developing self-awareness is about knowing exactly what lies within you. It is about becoming sensitive to yourself, your turmoil, your reactions, and your capabilities. Conscious awareness of yourself and these items can prevent your animal instincts from capturing your mind and keeping you from keeping your own discipline. Self-awareness can stop a knee jerk process in its tracks and bring your common sense back in control. Strongly developed self-awareness is important when considering and focusing on self-discipline. Developing self-awareness requires the management of your attention and strengths. Focus on becoming aware of your own patterns and triggers.

The Law of Awareness states, "You must know yourself to grow yourself." It's important that you know who you are on the inside in order to grow your own self-discipline. Self-discipline is about impulse control. Being self-aware is about being aware of your own impulses that you need to control. Animals are fully driven by instinct, but as humans we have a choice and we do not have to follow our instincts. However, in order to be able to control these instincts and ourselves, we must be fully aware of our own impulses.

Being aware of yourself is about seeing consequences for your instincts. You are not your impulses. Here are some things you can do to work on your own self-awareness:

- Journal
- Read
- Take Notes
- Figure Out What your Instincts Are

- Learn What your Triggers Are
- Talk to Your Family and Friends about Your Goals
- Focus on Yourself
- Think About Your Actions Before You Take them
- Think about the consequences to potential actions and goals
- Keep an open mind
- Be Mindful of your Strengths and Weaknesses
- Set Boundaries for yourself

Step 2: Being Your True Self

You have taken the time to be self-aware, but now you must focus on being your true self. Self-discipline is nothing if you cannot be the you that you are meant to be. Discover what your passions, strengths, values, and desires are. Believe in yourself as a person. You cannot develop any strong sense of self-discipline if you do not have a sense of yourself as a person. Your goals and desires for your self-discipline must align with who you are or your values and instincts will keep you from accomplishing your goals as a disciplined person.

Once you start searching for yourself, you will find that gaining a sense of who you are is the best knowledge that you will ever acquire. Your ability to fulfill your unique internal passion will determine your ability to realize your own potential. When you realize your potential, you can determine your quality and purpose in life. Determining your quality and purpose in life is easy to be determined. You can build self-discipline easy here. Here are questions you can ask yourself to determine your true self and desires. It is in this way and with these questions you can begin to build up your own self-discipline.

1. What do I love absolutely?

2. What do I consider my greatest accomplishments in life?

3. What would be my purpose if I knew no one would judge me?

4. If there were no limits to what I could have or could want in my life, what would that be?

5. If I had all the money in the world, what would I do?

6. Who do I admire most? Why do I admire this person the most?

Take the time to respond to these questions as you work to develop your own self-discipline. When you choose to implement your passions, strengths, values, desires and your motivations into your daily patterns, your life will become sweeter and the search for self-discipline will become easier. The question of how to become your true self and live most authentically is one that pertains to every aspect of our lives.

What kind of a person are you?

Step 3: Setting Goals to Maximize Your Ability

Having goals for things we want to do and working towards them is an important part of being human. Having strong goals is vital to having good self-discipline. The path towards your goals may not always be easy. Having goals, whether big or small, is part of what makes life good. Without your goals which create a sense of purpose, it is impossible to have good self-discipline.

Over 2000 years ago, Aristotle said "Well begun is half done." Aristotle was onto something here. Something that will help you with all of your self-discipline goals. Without goals, you cannot have motivation, power, and self-discipline. Paying attention to how you set your goals will make you likely to achieve them. Achieving goals makes you feel better about yourself and makes you want to keep going and pursuing.

Decide.

Think of something you want to do or work towards: decide on something for yourself. It doesn't matter what, as long as it's something you want to do. It should be something you want to do for its own sake and for yourself not for something or someone else. It can be a big thing or a small thing. You can stretch yourself a bit with this goal. Don't be afraid.

Write it down.

Carefully. Writing down your goals increases your chances of completing them. Write down how you will know you have reached your goals and when you'd like to have achieved it by. Ask yourself: what it will 'look' like and how will you feel when you've done it? How does it connect to who or what you value in your life?

Describe your goal in specific terms and timescales. Be specific and set small increments in the goal. Write your goals in terms of what you want, not what you don't want. Set small achievable goals.

Tell someone.

Telling someone you know about your goals also seems to increase the likelihood that you will stick at them.

Break your goal down.

Breaking your goal down is vitally important and even more needed for big goals. Think about the smaller goals that are steps on the way to achieving your bigger goal. Sometimes our big goals are a bit vague. Do not just choose "I want to be healthier." Instead, break it down, to specific small weight loss and food/health goals. Breaking these down helps us be more specific. Write down your smaller goals and set some dates to do these by. Having several smaller goals makes each of them a bit easier and gives us a feeling of success along the way. Success makes self-discipline feel more real. Success makes self-discipline easier.

Plan your first step.

An ancient Chinese proverb says that the journey of 1000 miles starts with one step. The best way you can start is by taking the first step. If you think about goals in-terms of steps, you may find that it is easier. Even if you don't know where to start there's no excuse. Your first step could be to research. Look up or ask someone what your first step should or could be. Go to the library. Get started. If you have self-discipline, you will discover that there is no step you cannot take. Having this knowledge will make your entire life and your motivation is better.

Keep going.

Working towards our goals can sometimes be difficult and frustrating. Keep going and persevere. Writing down your goals is not all it takes to develop self-discipline. Consider different ways of reaching your goals. If you are really stuck on something try and break it down further or take a break and start again later. When you finish, think about what you learned and how you can utilize it for the next goals that you have. If you keep this process up, it will go better.

Set SMART Goals

The simple fact is that for goals to be powerful, they should be designed to be SMART. There are many variations of what SMART stands for, but the essence is this:

Specific.

Measurable.

Attainable.

Relevant.

Time Bound.

Set Specific Goals

Your goal must be clear and well defined. Vague goals are unhelpful because they don't provide good direction. Remember, you need goals to show you the way. Make it as easy as you can to get where you want to go by defining precisely where you want to end up.

Tips

- Frame your goals positively.
- Keep your goals at the top of your to-do list
- Post your goals in visible places that you will always see.
- Make and keep an action plan
- Keep individual steps and cross them off as you go
- Keep goal setting active. Do not just do it once and call it good.

Step 4: Being Honest with Yourself

Being honest with yourself is one of the most important aspects of having self-discipline. It is your responsibility to know who you are, what you are capable of, and what you are supposed to be doing. Maybe you are deceiving yourself into believing that your career or relationship is great, when it's not. It's possible that you beat yourself up over your goals, when you're actually doing a great job. Either way, being honest with yourself is a great opportunity to build life skills, rise above challenges, gain self-acceptance, and improve authenticity. You bust be honest with yourself unless you want to lose your ability to have self-discipline.

The question of how to improve your own self honesty is a difficult one. This can be one of the most difficult hurdles you must cross in order to become self-disciplined. Here are the steps you can take to improve your own self honesty and thus, your self-discipline. It is in this way that you can work to keep yourself from lying to yourself. You do not have to convince yourself that you can do something later. Instead, you must work to know that you must get something done. Be honest with yourself about your desires and capabilities. Here are steps you can take to be honest with yourself. Follow these as much as necessary.

Step 1: Self Asses

Identify an area for self-evaluation. This can be anything as little as your cleaning habits and as big as your partner.

Be courageous. Pick a place to start that will give you a leg up, but that you know you are capable of.

Set some time aside for yourself. Take the time to be the person that you can be. Meditate. Think through things in your simple stuff.

Write everything down. Answer questions about yourself. Write down your strengths and weaknesses. Think about what areas undermine your success. What is holding you back? What are you doing for yourself? What is keeping you and suggesting that you hold yourself back?

Step 2: Review and act on your self-assessment.

Find where you need improvement and where you excel.

Do not give up. Fight against these things that hold you back.

Ask your friends how they see you. Ask your friends to help you.

Step 3: Chart your progress

Step 4: Celebrate your rewards.

Tips for being honest with yourself:
- Remember, there is no harm in writing something down. You can choose not to share it, destroy it, edit it, or simply keep it a secret.
- If you don't know where to begin, try taking a personality test. They cannot discover you by themselves, but they can lend some insight about your nature to help get you started. Perhaps a test can help you begin to understand and be honest with yourself.
- If you do not know what you want, seek outside help. Take a test, talk to a counselor, ask your friends.

- You can always seek professional help no matter what progress you are making. Being honest with yourself doesn't mean you have to work alone.

Step 5: Find Your Motivation

Self-discipline and dedication takes motivation. In fact, as far as self-discipline goes, motivation has a positive relationship. The more you find and focus on motivation, the more you receive self-discipline traits. The more focus and work on self-discipline, the more you gain motivation and drive to continue to work.

Motivation can be difficult to find sometimes. It can hide away from us and feel totally worthless. Even those people who are the most motivated and self-disciplined can lost motivation at times. In fact, sometimes we get into such a slump that even thinking about making positive changes seems too difficult.

Motivation is not hopeless. With some small steps you can get started down the road to positive change. It can seem impossible at times. Remember that you are not alone. Here are some helpful tools to focus on motivation. Here are some things you can do to continue on and help to build your motivation:

1. **One Goal**. You can always do your other goals when you've accomplished your One Goal. Pick one and take it from there. If you can do one thing, you can do the next thing and on and on.

2. **Find inspiration**. Look to the internet, your friends, your family, animals, and books. Find something that inspires you. Find something that helps push you.

3. **Get excited**.

4. **Build anticipation**. This will sound hard, and many people will skip this tip. But it really works. If you

find inspiration and want to do a goal, don't start right away. Set a date in the future — a week or two, or even a month — and make that your Start Date. Mark it on the calendar. This is a great way to get excited about the future. Get excited about that date. Make it the most important date in your life at this time. Start writing out a plan. By delaying your start, you are building anticipation, and increasing your focus and energy for your goal.

5. **Post your goal**. Print out your goal in big words. Write it where you will see it over and over again. Keep it posted and reminding you. Keep it positive with good motivation.

6. **Commit publicly**. Tell your friends and family what you are doing. Let others know what you are

doing. You will be more motivated if you find yourself support.

7. **Get support**. It's hard to accomplish something alone. Find your support network, either in the real world or online, or both. This will give you more motivation and help. Support, friends, and family make great motivators. They will be proud of you This proud feeling gives you more motivation and help. It gives you even more to look forward to when you are done.

8. **Stick with it**. Whatever you do, don't give up. Even if you aren't feeling any motivation today, or this week, don't give up. Again, that motivation will come back. Know that it will be back and stronger than ever when you know.

9. **Build on small successes**.

10. **Read about it daily**. Utilize blogs. Ask the internet and books for assistance. Read about other people taking advantage of and utilizing their skills. Read about the self-discipline of others. Read about how other people are doing. Read about what the others Read about how great it is when others succeed with the same success you are hoping to gain later.

11. **Call for help when your motivation ebbs**. Having trouble? Ask for help. Call your friends and family. Look online.

12. **Think about the benefits, not the difficulties**. Think about and focus on what good things will happen once you finish your goals. This is great motivation.

13. **Squash negative thoughts; replace them with positive ones**. Positivity breeds positivity. Do not allow negative thoughts to permeate your being. Let them work for you. Being positive can make all of the difference for you and those around you.

Step 6: Develop Your Will Power

Willpower is an important muscle that you must keep up and keep working well. Will power be important in self-discipline? Will power and self-discipline is important and vital to leading a happy and healthy life. Will power be like a muscle: it must be worked to be sustained, but it can be overworks, strained, and injured. Take the time to strengthen and work on your willpower and you will see a positive result in your self-discipline. Will power is needed for self-discipline, self-discipline is needed for will power?

Here are some things you can do to help strengthen your will power and in-turn, work on your self-discipline:

1) Don't overwork your willpower.

Many people use weight lifting to build their muscle, but they make sure they do not overwork them. You must do the same for your will power. Exercise your self-control and will power regularly. This strengthens it and, in turn, strengthens your self-discipline. However, make sure that you do not constantly deprive yourself or hurt your own willpower. This will just make things worse. Do not burn yourself out. If you burn yourself out, you will only make your self-confidence completely dwindle.

2) Use your imagination.

Imagination is a powerful technique for improving willpower. Your body is sure to respond to imagined situations in the same way it responds to experienced ones. If you imagine standing in snow when you are trying to cool down while doing something hot, you will be able to continue to work hard in the hot areas. Use this in your advantage as you work on building your will power and your self-confidence. Think about something else.

3) Build good habits for yourself.

If you keep working hard and building up your will power like a muscle, that good habit will work out will for you in the end. When you get stressed out, these habits will serve you well. Practice makes perfect, even in self-discipline and will power.

4) Be yourself

5) Stay away from temptations

There is no point in tempting yourself when you do not need it. If you are trying to avoid candy, do not go into a candy shop.

Willpower can be one of your greatest strengths. It can give you the ability to keep going even when you think the odds are impossible. Willpower separates your abilities from animal instincts. It is not simply about living, but it is about doing everything that you are capable of. It is about pushing yourself and accomplishing your goals. Willpower is so very helpful and powerful. Remember to keep your willpower up for your own abilities. Will power is crucial in self-discipline.

Step 7: Break Old Habits

Bad habits suck. A bad habit can ruin your entire set of goals and your entire strategy to do better. In order to improve your personal well-being and self-discipline, in order to have a better life with better success, you must first break down your old, bad habits. You must break down the issues that are associated with your lack of self-control. Break down your regular de-stressors and select new ones. It is in this way that you will find success. Breaking down a bad habit takes at least 21 days. Our bodies were meant for repetition and consistency. Do not continue to live a mundane life. Utilize these tips honestly to focus on getting yourself out of the old, bad habits and into a better system of habits and self-discipline.

- Fine yourself for each offense. You will be less likely to continue the bad habit if you have to pay for doing it. Pick a jar and put money in it when you do not do your best. Adversely, reward yourself when you are able to control those desires to continue the habit.

- Focus on understanding what triggers your bad habits. Understanding how we make decisions is the key to conquering all kinds of bad habits. If you focus on understanding why your habits are bad, you will better me able to figure out how to beat them and turn them into better ones. Self-discipline requires that you understand your bad habits and your bad desires in order to be stronger for them. Often, we repeat bad habits without even realize we're doing them.

- Go slow and make little changes. Take your time. Much like with will power, you do not want to overdo it. Take the time to make the right changes in the right way for you.

- Set reminders in your calendar. Remind yourself to stay strong. Be good to yourself.

- Change your environment. Sometimes in order to change your habits you need to change your environment. If you are struggling to work, try working somewhere else. Your self disciple will thank you.

- Try to find some new habits. Find better ways to spend your time.

Step 8: Cultivate New Habits

You cannot expect anything but instinct to stand behind you when you get stressed or when issues face you. Breaking down old, bad habits is the first step to cultivating these new habits that will help you with self-discipline. Building a good habit takes at least 21 days of hard work. We all have areas in our lives where we want to improve. So set goals and turn those goals into new routines which will then turn into habits. You might fail, but do not let that discourage you.

Often, you may start out on a good foot trying to make a new habit, but it does not always stick. You can fail and falter after just a few days. Generally, it is said that it takes 21 days to make a habit stick, but it can take anywhere from 18 to 254 days. This can be a total discouragement. It is important that you persevere while you work on your new habits.

Understand that habits can seem overwhelming. Try your hardest to focus not on the overly large aspect of the habit, but instead on the small victories and daily works of habits. Focus on your routine each day and it will get better.

When looking at a habit, there are three parts that make a habit stick:

    A cue

    A routine

    A reward

The cue reminds you to do the habit. The routine is what you do automatically. The reward is the payoff you get by doing the routine. This will get better and better as time goes on. Understanding the three keys to a habit makes it easier to take on your habits.

When creating good habits, you have to do the same thing over and over. This may sound boring to you, but you have to stick with the same routine if you want to turn the routine into a habit. If you change things up, you will never associate the reward with the routine and therefore the routine will never become a habit. Make this an important experience to accept as you take on these challenges.

Building these habits can seem scary and difficult. Recognize that sometimes failure happens. Sometimes you will lose. That is okay. Just make sure that you pick yourself back up and get going again. The more you keep trying over and over again, the better you will be for it. Give yourself motivation and effort. Everything in this book plays off of itself. The way in which you will do well is to remember that.

A good habit will help you when self-discipline and planning fails. Sometimes stuff is more difficult than we anticipate. Sometimes there are stressors that make it seem harder to keep going. However, in these times, our bodies will still remember our habits. If you still remember the habits that you work hard to develop, you will still be able to practice strong self-discipline.

Step 9: Track Your Progress

Journaling is so very important if you are trying to develop your own self-discipline. You need to keep track of your progress, how it makes you feel, what you failed at, and what you succeeded at. Stay strong with your goals and everything else. The best way to do this is to get your own journal. Self-discipline is nothing if you do not know yourself. If you track your progress and pay attention to what you are doing, you will find that self-discipline is easier to come by. This type of progress tracking can be done in so many different ways. Utilize charts and figured to show yourself what kind of progress you are making on a specific goal. Ask your friends and families to hold you accountable.

You can keep track of habits and multi-day goals by utilizing a system of dots or marking days off of calendars.

You might try having two jars with rocks in one. As you complete your goal each day you can move one rock to the empty jar. It is in this way that you can slowly see the progress shifting and moving. You will see that this change happens slowly, but on each day you make a difference. Each day the work will change what is in the jars.

If you choose to journal and write down your progress, which I suggest you do, I suggest you look at these journal questions. Use them as a great way to get a sense of yourself and figure out what type of work you need to do to increase your self-discipline.

- What do you think self-discipline is? How do you feel about self-discipline?
- What does practicing self-discipline mean for you?
- How do you want self-discipline to help you?
- Are you self-aware?

- What are your instincts?
- What are your triggers?
- What are your strengths?
- What are your weaknesses?

- Do you feel like you know your true self?
    - Have you asked your friends or family?
    - Take a personality test: How do you feel about the results?

- What are your goals?

- Are you honest with yourself?
    - What is it that you most need? What areas are you the most dishonest with yourself in?
    - What areas are you the most honest in?

- Where do you find your motivation?

- What is your will power?

    o How do you build your will power?

- What old habits do you need to break?
- What new habits do you want to build?

    o How will you build them?

Here are some daily questions you can answer to help build your self-discipline up:

- What do you want to accomplish today?
- Do you feel self-disciplined all day? Only part of the day?
- How did you encourage yourself today? Did it work well?

Keeping track of your progress tells you well where you are at. It keeps you on track and encourages your self-discipline. It helps push you forward. This is important if you want your self-discipline to stay strong and your abilities to improve.

10 Day Challenge

Rewards for Being Self-Disciplined

Self-discipline is a way of life. When you are self-disciplined, you live systematically and with a strength that moves mountains. Self-disciplined is not just about money, or abilities. Self-discipline is about finding and capturing a better life. It is about finishing everything you start. Self-discipline is a habit of forming and working on good habits. Many successful people claim they are famous or successful because they have strong self-discipline.

Self-discipline is about being focused, staying healthy and also avoiding problems. A strong self-discipline technique is a strong social skill.

Here are some advantages you will experience from having a strong sense of self-discipline.

Focus: Being disciplined helps you stay focused on your work, goals, and objectives. If you have strong, focused goals, you will keep that focus through everything.

Respect: The most respected men and women of all time had strong self-discipline. Self-discipline naturally commands respect from others. If you struggle to gain the respect of others, you have not earned it with your self-discipline and strength of will.

Stay Active and Healthy: If your life is self-disciplined it will have regular habits like eating the right food, staying clean and taken care of, waking and sleeping at right time. When you exercise and practice other great habits you will be well taken care of and happier. Self-discipline gives you the structure necessary to make a fantastic difference with everything that you do, especially your own self-care. People who are well disciplined are always more active than others. They tend to stay active the whole day. Being active and healthy has its own benefits of increased happiness and pleasure. With this, you will live longer and do more.

Self-control: If you have a stronger self-discipline, you will have better control over yourself. You will be able to control potential rash instincts when people rub you the wrong way. You will be able to keep yourself from eating the things you know you should not be eating. Discipline comes with self-control. This will increase your relations with other people and make everything in your life slightly better and more peaceful. Those people who are the most successful in life also have the best amounts of self-discipline and self-control.

More learning: Strong self-discipline can lead to more learning and a better, stronger education. Those people who can decide to allow themselves to constantly learn and be disciplined will be pleasantly surprised by their abilities. Self-discipline in the classroom can help students to listen to teachers and other things that are covered in the class well. Homework and learning is better and stronger.

Productivity and Happiness: Being disciplined helps get things done faster and in right amount of time. It is very important that those who focus on discipline are also happy and productive: it makes the discipline easier. Being happy and productive tells you that what you are doing (practicing self-discipline) is the right thing for you. This type of productivity and happiness can lead to peace of mind. Staying up with self-discipline can change the productivity, happiness, and healthiness of personal relationships as well.

If you want to see your friendships improve, your relationships function better, and your friends and family with more smiles on their faces, focus on self-discipline as a tool.

Less Stress: Self-discipline comes with less stress and tension. If you do not know what you should expect each day and do not have a disciplined action plan for taking care of yourself, you will develop fear and anxiety. A stronger sense of self-discipline will give you more power over your ability to have stress. Self-discipline helps to develop self-esteem and strength.

Ten Day Start Plan for Self-Discipline

If you are still having a hard time getting your life together and disciplined, this may be the section for you.

This ten-day plan provides a perfect platform to get started on your improved life with. After following this plan, you will begin to reap the rewards of a job well done. You will be less stressed and gain more motivation. Self-discipline is a lot like a muscle. You must consistently work it out. When you are finished with this ten-day plan, that is not the end of the road. You must continuously work on your self-discipline. Create your own plans and goals as time goes on. Do not be afraid to reach out to your friends and family for support and help. You will be for the better once you begin to work on yourself and your discipline.

Day 1: Evaluate yourself. Your Strengths, and Your Weaknesses.

Figure what you can and cannot do. Become as self-aware as you possibly can. Write it down and evaluate it. What does it mean? What can you do about it? How do you feel about it?

Day 2: Practice To-do Lists

Set small goals in the form of a to-do list and accomplish them. Make sure you know that you should be proud of yourself. You are practicing self-discipline.

Day 3: Get motivated.

Make a list of all of the reasons you want to change. Think about the people that encourage you. Find your motivation and self-discipline will fall into line.

Day 4: Make a plan.

Make a plan for what you want to do with your life. Plan what you want to get done. Write it down. Be realistic. Set your goals.

Day 5: Get rid of bad habits.

List bad habits you want to get rid of and begin working on them. Bad habits can ruin your self-discipline. Begin working on them now. This will take some time, but it will begin to make you feel better.

Day 6: Make it public.

Tell your friends and family about your goals. They will be able to encourage you. When you tell other people, you will find that you have more motivation and are more likely to keep going.

Day 7: New habits.

Decide on some new habits and routines you want to instill in yourself. Make sure you are developing habits that go along with your goals.

Day 8: Empower yourself through change.

Every time you make a positive step towards building self-discipline, no matter how small, recognize how empowering it is. Admit and acknowledge that it feels good to be a positive change.

Day 9: Evaluate your progress.

You have been doing well so far. Look at how you are doing. Evaluate how it makes you feel. This is a very important part of the process. Make sure that you make changes accordingly.

Day 10: Reward yourself.

Congratulations! You have done a great job! Reward yourself for being great at self-discipline. Keep going!

Conclusion: Enjoy Your New Self-discipline

Having good self-discipline is awesome! I hope you use this guide well and take advantage of what you are capable of as a human. Remember, you are more than instincts and reactions. You have the power to be totally self-aware. You, as a self-disciplined human can push past your instincts and impressively take advantage of your humanity. Take advantage of your strengths. With self-discipline you can minimize your weaknesses and turn them into even more strengths. It is time that you work to discover your true self. Decide who you want to be. Take the time to format smart goals that you can accomplish. Focus and dedicate yourself. Reward yourself for doing well. Self-discipline can quickly show you the ways to find your motivation and your voice. Congratulations on starting this new journey! Remember that self-discipline is a great way to get done everything that you want.

www.ingramcontent.com/pod-product-compliance
Lightning Source LLC
Chambersburg PA
CBHW070404190526
45169CB00003B/1110